ASTIC FREE
ASTLINES
ERS AGAINST SEWAGE

e child, one teacher, one book and one pen
can change the world
MALALA YOUSAFZAI

HONOR KING: END RACISM!

Man needs rain forests too
The tropical rain forests are home to half of all the
plant animal and insect species on earth, and are
watersheds that prevent erosion drought and flooding.
Help WWF save them from destruction.

WWF 🐼 WORLD WILDLIFE FUND Panda House 11-13 Ockford Road Godalming Surrey

PROTECT KIDS

The
hungry
need
bread
not
bombs

Stop the
arms
trade

DONT SHOOT

NOT GUNS

WOMEN AGAINST APARTHEID

support the struggle
of women
of the liberation
movements
anc and swapo

SOME PEOPLE ARE GAY.
GET OVER IT!

www.stonewall.org.uk

⭐ **Stonewall**
Acceptance without exception

STAND TOGETHER
CND
EASTER
1983

Burghfield
Aldermaston
Greenham
Thursday 31st March

MAKE TEA NOT WAR

STOP THE
WAR
COALITION

ZA EVROPU MIRU - BEZ JADERNÝCH ZBRANÍ

NO DRAFT
NO WAR
NO
NO

NO BAN NO WALL

AMNESTY
INTERNATIONAL

FOR ZACH AND LEO

Every effort has been made to trace the copyright holders and obtain permission to reproduce this material. For the kind permission to reproduce the images in this book, the Publishers would like to thank: **Alamy**: page 12 Pictorial Press Ltd; page 13 The Protected Art Archive; page 22 Contraband Collection; pages 25, 30, 33 World History Archive; page 28 Mark Phillips. **Amnesty International**: page 8 (USA); page 15 (Egypt); back cover and page 20 (USA); page 21 (Ireland); page 46 (UK); page 54 (UK); page 59 (Switzerland); Walker Agency page 61 (USA). **Black Lives Matter**: pages 26–27. **Loui Brezzell**: page 7 Mari Copeny. **Bridgeman Images**: back cover and page 18 Gilder Lehrman Collection; page 52 © ADAGP, Paris and DACS, London 2019; page 55 American School (20th century). **Lisa Congdon**: page 40. Page 58 **Image courtesy of Sam Eckersley and World Wildlife Fund UK**. With thanks to the University of the Arts London Archives and Special Collections Centre. **Fondation Émergence**: page 51. **Victoria García**: page 16. **Getty Images**: page 10 Heritage Images; page 23 photo by MPI/Getty Images; pages 34 and 35 Universal History Archive/UIG; pages 42–43 photo by API/Gamma-Rapho. **Matt Huynh**: page 39. **Memac Ogilvy & Mather Dubai**: page 17. **Micah Bazant**: page 36. **OMCA Collections**: page 31 (AOUON Archive) courtesy Lincoln Cushing. **Private Collection**: back cover and page 24. **Rex Shutterstock**: page 38 Granger. **Stonewall**: page 44. **Surfers Against Sewage**: pages 56–57. **Syracuse Cultural Workers and SyracuseCulturalWorkers.com**: page 14 International Women's Day 100 Years poster by Favianna Rodriguez; page 41 Malala Yousafzai, with art by Vecteezy.com; page 47 Come Out Come Out; page 49 Stonewall 25 Illustration by Harry Freeman-Jones; page 50 A Little Too Straight, with art by Laurie Casagrande. **Rommy Torrico**: page 48. **UNHCR**: page 32 courtesy of LEGO Group.

2020 First US edition
Text copyright © 2019 by Palazzo Editions Limited
Design copyright © 2019 by Palazzo Editions Limited
Jacket illustrations copyright © 2020 by Jacqueline Noelle Cote
Foreword copyright © 2020 by Mari Copeny. All rights reserved.

A portion of the royalties from the sale of this book will be donated to Amnesty International.

Published by Charlesbridge
85 Main Street
Watertown, MA 02472
(617) 926-0329
www.charlesbridge.com

First published in Great Britain in 2019 by Palazzo Editions Limited, 15 Church Road, London SW13 9HE
www.palazzoeditions.com

Library of Congress Cataloging-in-Publication Data available upon request.
ISBN 978-1-62354-150-7 (reinforced for library use)
ISBN 978-1-63289-949-1 (ebook)
ISBN 978-1-63289-950-7 (ebook pdf)

Printed in China
(hc) 10 9 8 7 6 5 4 3 2 1

Hand-lettering by Jacqueline Noelle Cote
Display type set in Buntaro by David Kerkhoff
Text type set in ITC Franklin Gothic by Adobe Systems Inc. and Colby by Jason Vandenberg
Color separations by XY Digital in the UK
Printed by C&C Offset Printing Ltd in China
Production supervision by Brian G. Walker

JO RIPPON

RISE UP!

THE ART OF PROTEST

In collaboration with
AMNESTY INTERNATIONAL

Foreword by
MARI COPENY

🏛 Charlesbridge

CONTENTS

FOREWORD

Activism. Most kids have no idea what this word means. I had no idea what it meant, even when what I was doing was activism. But now activism is a part of who I am. It's a part of who we are as a society. When we see an injustice in the world and stand up and speak out to change it, that's activism.

Youth activists have been at the forefront of many movements. From Black Lives Matter to the fight against climate change, kids today are stepping up and speaking out because we know that the world is ours, too. If we don't help fix the mess that people are making now, it will be way harder for us to fix it in the future.

Today's youth are more connected and more aware of what's going on around us than ever before. We're able to coordinate with others from across the country and build platforms to bring change to the world.

No more sitting around and waiting for the adults to fix things. No more letting our elected politicians make decisions about our lives. It's time for us to speak up for ourselves because it's our present, and our future, that are at stake.

—Mari Copeny

In 2014 officials in Flint, Michigan, switched the city's water source from Lake Huron to the Flint River. The improperly treated river water ate away at pipes, causing dangerous chemicals to leach into the water. Thousands of children were exposed to dangerously high levels of lead.

In 2016 eight-year-old Mari Copeny wrote a letter to President Barack Obama about the Flint water crisis. President Obama responded to Mari's letter and visited the city. Mari told him, "You know, I wrote to you!" The president replied, "I know! That's why I decided to come." Thanks in part to Mari's efforts, the federal government granted $100 million to Flint to upgrade its water system.

Today Mari "Little Miss Flint" Copeny continues to raise awareness of Flint's struggle to recover from the water crisis. She has also raised more than $500,000 to help the city's children.

INTRODUCTION

> Never doubt that a small group of thoughtful, committed citizens can change the world. Indeed, it is the only thing that ever has.
>
> *Attributed to Margaret Mead, anthropologist and activist*

One Movement, One Message, Many Voices

Amnesty International
1988, USA

Featuring artwork by Seymour Chwast, this poster commemorates the fortieth anniversary of the Universal Declaration of Human Rights.

Protest is not a new idea. It might seem that way because of recent high-profile marches, rallies, and demonstrations. But throughout history there are many examples of people coming together to try to make the world a better and fairer place. This book shows how protest has helped inspire change, from the early suffragists who fought for equal voting rights for women to the more recent youth activists who have walked out of classrooms to oppose climate change.

Looking at six key areas of protest, *Rise Up! The Art of Protest* brings together some of the different and creative ways in which people from around the world have made their voices heard. From hand-printed posters to social media campaigns, creativity can be a positive way to deal with feelings of anger and frustration when things are unfair. It can also be a captivating way of getting others to listen.

A protest can be about a local issue, such as the closing of a library, or it can be about a larger problem, such as racism, environmental destruction, or war. What's important is that protesting is a way to stand up for what you think is right. Not everybody has this opportunity. There are places in the world where it can be hard, or even impossible, to speak out about injustice. Protesting is also a way of showing support to others and uniting us to make the world a better place for everyone.

Heraus mit dem Frauenwahlrecht
FRAUEN-TAG/
8. MÄRZ 1914

Den Frauen, die als Arbeiterinnen, Mütter und Gemeindebürgerinnen ihre volle Pflicht erfüllen, die im Staat wie in der Gemeinde ihre Steuern entrichten müssen, hat Voreingenommenheit und reaktionäre Gesinnung das volle Staatsbürgerrecht bis jetzt verweigert.

Dieses natürliche Menschenrecht zu erkämpfen, muß der unerschütterliche, feste Wille jeder Frau, jeder Arbeiterin sein. Hier darf es kein Ruhen kein Rasten geben. Kommt daher alle, ihr Frauen und Mädchen in die am

Sonntag den 8. März 1914 nachmittags 3 Uhr stattfindenden
9 öffentl. Frauen-Versammlungen

WOMEN'S RIGHTS ARE HUMAN RIGHTS

> ❝ The story of women's struggle for equality belongs to no single feminist nor to any one organization but to the collective efforts of all who care about human rights. ❞
>
> *Gloria Steinem, feminist, journalist, and activist*

Heraus mit dem Frauenwahlrecht (Give Us Women's Suffrage)

Designed by Karl Maria Stadler
1914, Germany

This poster calls on people to join a Women's Day march being held on March 8, 1914, to demand the right of women to vote in Germany. The suffrage movement became popular across Europe at the beginning of the last century. In Germany women were granted the right to vote on November 12, 1918. March 8 has become known as International Women's Day and is an opportunity for women to voice their demands.

For many hundreds of years, in many cultures, if you were born rich and male, you had the right to vote, buy a house, or inherit money from your family. If you were born female, you had no say in who passed the laws in the country where you lived.

In 1792 English writer Mary Wollstonecraft wrote a book called *A Vindication of the Rights of Woman*. She argued that society was unfair and that women should have the same rights as men. Many people consider her book the start of Western feminism.

Around the world women (and some men) began to demand equal voting rights. They became known as the suffragettes. In 1893 New Zealand became the first country to grant women the right to vote.

World War I was a turning point for women's rights. With the men away fighting, the women worked in offices, factories, and fields, helping to keep their countries running. Their efforts made it almost impossible for governments to refuse them a say in how things were run. Gradually northern Europe, Britain, and the United States followed New Zealand and gave women the right to vote.

Other governments still resisted. For many women, gaining the right to vote was a long and hard battle. France finally allowed women to vote in 1944, Japan in 1947, Mexico in 1953, and the Bahamas in 1961. In South Africa it wasn't until 1994 that all women could vote. The most recent country to allow women to vote was Saudi Arabia, in 2015.

But this isn't the end. Many women are still paid less than men for doing the same work, and in some parts of the world women do not even have basic rights to freedom, education, or health care. Over the years the struggle for equality has grown to include these issues. There is an increasing belief that women's rights should not be seen as separate from human rights—after all, women make up half the world's population.

Let Ohio Women Vote

Designed by Cornelia Cassady Davis
c. 1912, USA

This poster shows a young woman standing in front of three hilltops over which the sun is rising. On the right is a sheaf of wheat, which represents Ohio's farming industry, and on the left are arrows, a symbol of Native American heritage.

In the United States, many people campaigned to change their state's laws that prevented women from voting. The Ohio Woman Suffrage Association was unusual because it was one of the few women's rights groups that actively encouraged African American women to join its cause. In 1920 the Nineteenth Amendment to the Constitution was ratified. It states that the right to vote in the United States cannot be denied on the basis of sex.

Votes for Women

Designed by suffragette artist Hilda Dallas
1909, UK

This poster advertises *Votes for Women*, the official newspaper of the Women's Social and Political Union—in the suffragette colors of purple, white, and green.

100 Years of International Women's Day

Designed by Favianna Rodriguez
in collaboration with Syracuse
Cultural Workers
2010, USA

This poster celebrates one hundred
years of International Women's Day,
which was first held in Austria,
Denmark, Germany, and Switzerland
on March 19, 1911. Today it is
observed around the world on March
8, in recognition of the many
achievements of women, as well as
the continued demand for equality.
The female figure in the background
of this poster is Mother Earth and
represents all women everywhere.

Defenders of Women's Rights

Amnesty International
1994, Egypt

This poster by Amnesty International Egypt is part of an international campaign that proclaims "Human rights are women's rights." The photograph of the flower over the woman's face represents the need for the rights of women to be cared for and nourished.

Women in Egypt have a long history of fighting for equality against what many see as a patriarchal system, controlled by men. In recent years some of the most prominent campaigners have been threatened by the government and charged with false crimes in an attempt to deter them from challenging the system.

RESPETA MI EXISTENCIA O ESPERA RESISTENCIA

Respeta (Respect)

Designed by Victoria García for Amplifier
2017, USA

"Respeta" was chosen as one of the five winning designs that became the official posters for the 2017 Women's March on Washington. It was also used in similar marches around the world. The Women's March was in protest against comments made by President Donald Trump that many people felt disrespected women. This poster translates to "Respect my existence or expect resistance."

Women Should . . .

Designed by Memac Oglivy & Mather Dubai for UN Women 2013, worldwide

Part of a series, this poster is based on actual Google searches from March 9, 2013. The searches used Google's autocomplete function, which predicts what you might be looking for based on what other people have searched for before.

The results were shocking. Negative statements exposed sexist attitudes, proving that there is still plenty to do in the fight for equality. The campaign was popular on social media and was mentioned on Twitter twenty-four million times.

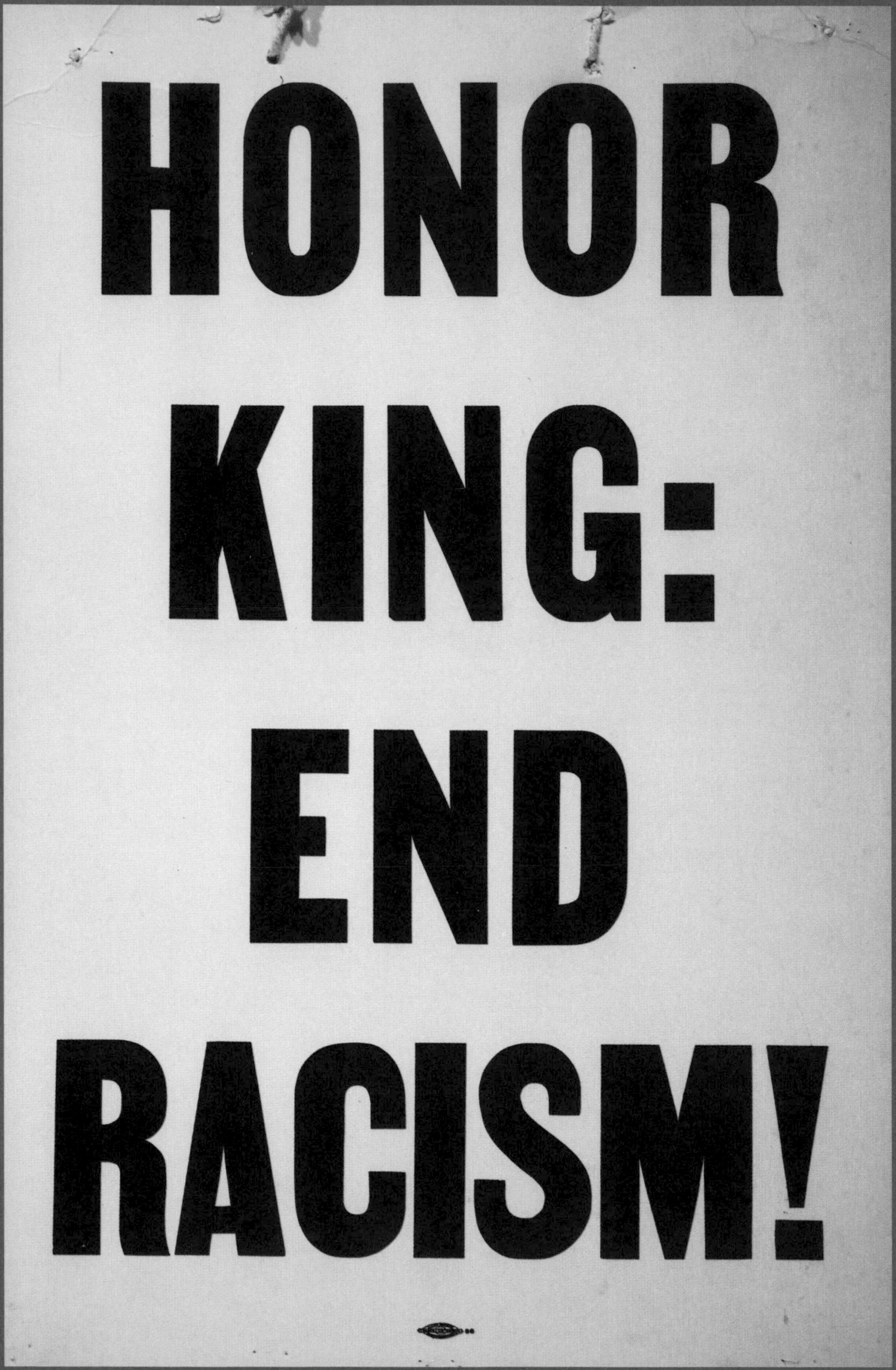
HONOR
KING:
END
RACISM!

OUR DIFFERENCES ARE ONLY SKIN DEEP

> "No one is born hating another person because of the colour of his skin, or his background, or his religion. People must learn to hate, and if they can learn to hate, they can be taught to love, for love comes more naturally to the human heart than its opposite. "

Nelson Mandela, first black president of South Africa

In ancient times people were divided based on their religion, social class, or language. Discrimination based on race didn't come into it. Race is a modern idea, and one that has resulted in people being treated unfairly.

Race was used to justify slavery in the United States. Supporters of slavery promoted the idea that because black people looked different from white people, it was acceptable to treat them differently. We now refer to this view as racism. Slavery was eventually abolished, but by then racist beliefs had become entrenched, and there were laws that favored one race over others.

There is a long history of protest against this injustice. Protesters in the civil rights movement fought against laws that denied black people basic rights such as education, housing, and jobs. They also sought to end segregation laws that separated black people from white people. There were "whites only" schools and housing areas, and white customers were served first in shops. Black people were not allowed to vote. Instead they protested to demand change.

During the 1950s and 1960s, protesters organized a series of peaceful demonstrations, forcing the nation to face the problems of racism. Activists Claudette Colvin and Rosa Parks refused to

Honor King: End Racism!

Allied Printing
1968, USA

Martin Luther King Jr. was one of the leaders of the civil rights movement in the United States. On April 8, 1968, four days after he was assassinated, his widow, Coretta Scott King, and three of her children led twenty thousand protesters in a peaceful march that honored his memory and called for an end to racism.

give up their bus seats to white people, leading to the Montgomery bus boycott. Martin Luther King Jr. and other civil rights leaders led more than two hundred thousand people in the March on Washington. Actions like these eventually led to the Civil Rights Act of 1964, which ended segregation and made it illegal to discriminate based on race.

There are many examples of one race of people oppressing and ruling over another. In Australia the Aboriginal people have suffered greatly under the rule of white colonizers; until 1967 they were not recognized as citizens of their own country and didn't count as part of the population. In South Africa a system of racial segregation called apartheid forced nonwhite people to live in separate areas and use separate schools, hospitals, and other facilities. Begun in 1948, apartheid was the law for more than forty-five years. It wasn't until 1994 that apartheid ended and the black population was allowed to vote for the first time.

People of all skin colors have the right to live freely and to be celebrated for the value and diversity they bring to the world. We can't undo history, but we can understand how events of the past have helped to shape a world where racism still exists.

Family Separations

Boys + Girls advertising agency with illustration by Noma Bar
2018, Ireland

Noma Bar, an Israeli graphic artist based in London, designed this poster for Amnesty International Ireland to protest family separations at the US-Mexico border. In 2017 the American government, led by President Trump, began removing thousands of children from their families as they tried to cross the border into the United States. The children were kept in prisonlike rooms, separated from their parents, for months. Trump has been very vocal about his dislike of immigration, and his views and actions are seen by many as racist and oppressive.

The image used in this poster is based on the American flag, a symbol of the "land of the free." The red stripes form the bars of a cage, through which a crying child looks out with a star for an eye.

No Ban, No Wall

Amnesty International
2017, USA

This poster protests two issues at the same time: a US travel ban that prevents people from several predominantly Muslim countries from entering the country, and the building of a wall between the United States and Mexico. Both are President Trump's policies and are seen as attacks on immigrants.

LIBERTAD PARA ANGELA DAVIS

Remember Wounded Knee

Designed by unknown artist
1973, USA

This poster commemorates the 1890 Wounded Knee Massacre, in which the US government killed hundreds of men, women, and children of the Lakota Sioux tribe. In 1973, protesters occupied the site of the massacre for seventy-one days to express their anger at the government's failure to honor its promises to Native American people.

Libertad para Angela Davis (Freedom for Angela Davis)

Designed by Félix Alberto Beltrán Concepción in Cuba;
replica by the New York Committee to Free Angela Davis
1971, USA

Angela Davis is a passionate civil rights activist. During the 1960s her outspokenness angered the US government, and in 1970 she was added to the FBI's most-wanted list, accused of kidnapping, murder, and criminal conspiracy. She was arrested on October 13, 1970. During her imprisonment, a "Free Angela" movement started to gather support. Davis was cleared of all charges on June 4, 1972.

THE *Spirit* of the past will rise to claim the FUTURE

WOUNDED KNEE.

IN THE MOON WHEN THE DEER SHED THEIR HORNS (DEC. 28, 1890)

MARCH 1973...

LIBERTAD PARA NELSON MANDELA Y TODOS LOS PRISONEROS POLITICOS DE SUD AFRICA   LIBEREZ NELSON MANDELA ET TOUS LES PRISONNIERS POLITIQUES DE L'AFRIQUE DU SUD

FREE NELSON MANDELA
AND ALL SOUTH AFRICAN POLITICAL PRISONERS

Free Nelson Mandela and All South African Political Prisoners

Designed by Rupert García for the Liberation Support Movement
1981, USA

Nelson Mandela was a South African activist who was jailed for protesting apartheid. He was what we call a political prisoner: someone imprisoned because they have criticized their government. Mandela was in prison for twenty-seven years, and people around the world campaigned for his freedom. His release led to the black population winning the right to vote. In 1994 Mandela became South Africa's first black president. Under his leadership, the government continued to dismantle the legacy of apartheid.

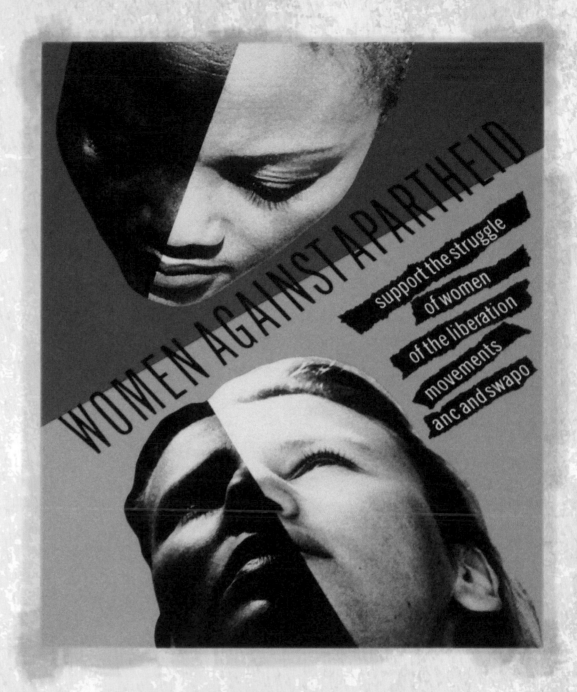

Women Against Apartheid

Designed by Lies Ros, Frank Beekers, and Rob Schröder
of Wild Plakken for the anti-apartheid movement
1984, Netherlands

Wild Plakken was a design group in the Netherlands. Its Dutch
name means "wild pasting" and refers to the way the group
pasted posters illegally around Amsterdam to draw attention
to political messages. The poster here features two female
heads, each with a dark-skinned half and a light-skinned half to
represent the conflict of the apartheid system.

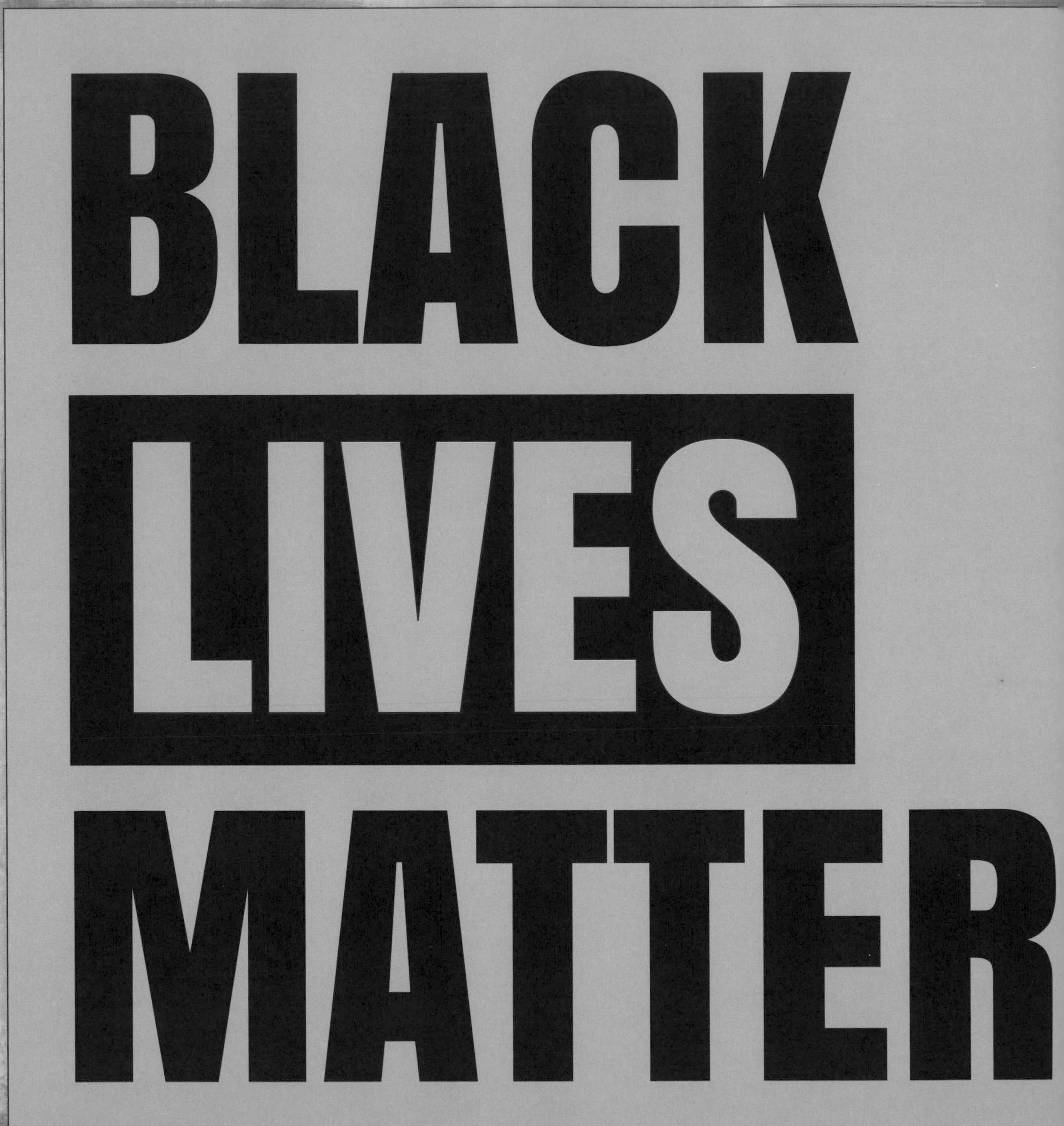
BLACK
LIVES
MATTER

WWW.BLACKLIVESMATTER.COM

Black Lives Matter

Design Action Collective
2013, USA

In 2012 a neighborhood watch member named George Zimmerman shot and killed black teenager Trayvon Martin. When Zimmerman was acquitted in 2013, activists Alicia Garza, Patrisse Cullors, and Opal Tometi started using the hashtag #BlackLivesMatter on Facebook and Twitter to campaign against violence toward black people. Now Black Lives Matter is a global network of more than forty member organizations.

THE FIGHT FOR PEACE

Make Tea Not War

Dave Buonaguidi for Karmarama
Photo: David H. Ramsey
2003, UK

This poster was created for an anti-war march held in London on February 15, 2003, to protest against the invasion of Iraq. Similar protests were held in more than six hundred cities worldwide on the same day. These protests have since been declared the "largest protest event in human history." The poster features a photograph of Tony Blair, the British prime minister at the time, holding a gun and wearing a teacup as a helmet.

As long as there have been wars, there have been people who object to them. But it wasn't always acceptable to protest against war, and to do so was seen by many people as unpatriotic. During World War I, people who refused to go to war were called conscientious objectors. It took courage to stand up and say no. Many of those who refused to fight were ridiculed, shamed, punished, or even sent to prison because of their peaceful beliefs.

After the destruction caused by the war, however, people became more open to the views of anti-war protesters. During the 1920s and 1930s, the peace movement gained in popularity—only to be interrupted by the start of another devastating war. After World War II ended in 1945, the call for peace regained momentum. Anti-war activists successfully paved the way for organizations such as the United Nations and the World Peace Council.

The 1960s and 1970s saw huge numbers of protests against war and nuclear weapons. The Vietnam War caused some of the biggest protests. The battle to bring an end to this war spread across the United States and the world. People openly expressed their opposition to the war and began questioning their governments in a way they had not before.

Despite the wish for world peace, war still happens. The world has been getting less peaceful. But it's important that we keep fighting for peace because history tells us that the cost of war is simply too great.

Campaign for Nuclear
Disarmament
1983, UK

On April 1, 1983, tens of
thousands of people linked
arms to form a "peace
chain" across what was
known as the Nuclear Valley
in the UK. The activists,
represented in this poster
by paper-doll cutouts, were
protesting against nuclear
activities in the area.

Peace is disarming

Drawing by Spencer Terry, Scotland. Published by the International Center of the World Peace. Council Lönnrotinkatu 25 A 5 fin-00180 Helsinki 18 Finland

Peace Is Disarming

Artwork by Spencer Terry for the
World Peace Council
1975, USA

The word *disarm* has two
meanings: to remove weapons and
to make something more likable
by removing suspicion. This poster
is using both of those meanings
to promote peace. It shows
children at the top of a castle, with
soldiers tied up below. One child
is discarding a cannonball, one
is placing flowers in the cannon,
and the third is releasing doves, a
symbol of peace.

PARASITE   **CRIMINAL**   **FOREIGN TRASH**   **PIG**

TROUBLEMAKER   **FREELOADER**   **VERMIN**   **SLACKER**

SCUM   **REFUGEE**   **YOU**   **ME**

WHAT'S THE DIFFERENCE?

Nasty names. Shocking even in print. But all too common if you're unlucky enough to be a refugee.

Wait. Why are "you" and "me" among them? And why is every figure identical? They're all the same!

Exactly!

You see, refugees *are* just like you and me. So what's the difference?

There's really only one: fear.

While our homes are safe and our rights are protected, their homes have been left behind and the rights they once enjoyed were swept away by violence and hatred. They've been living in constant fear for their lives.

That's why they've had to leave their country. That's why they are refugees. Of course they wish they were back home – wouldn't you? But it's still too dangerous, and for now we must continue to offer them our help.

So please, don't get mad at refugees.

Instead, save your breath for the situation that's *made* them refugees.

UNHCR

United Nations High Commissioner for Refugees

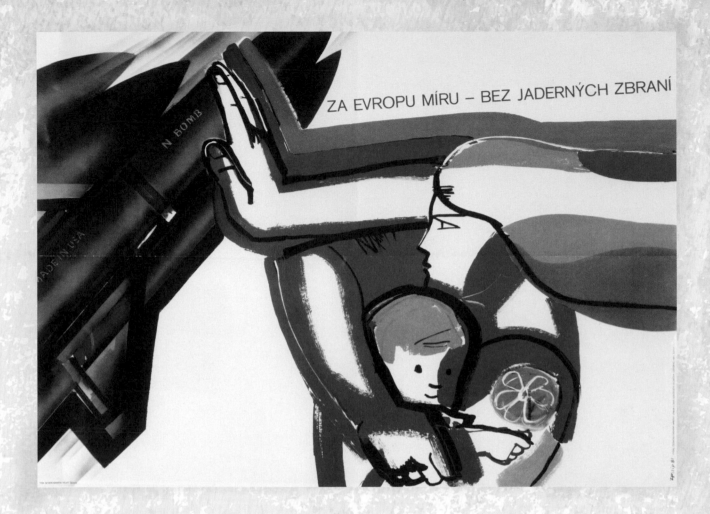

ZA EVROPU MÍRU – BEZ JADERNÝCH ZBRANÍ

What's the Difference?

UNHCR and the LEGO Group
1994–1997, worldwide

War causes other problems. In 1950 the office of the United Nations High Commissioner for Refugees (UNHCR) was created to help the millions of people displaced from their homes due to World War II. Today there are more than 65 million forcibly displaced people worldwide—the biggest number ever.

In 1993 the UNHCR approached the LEGO Group for permission to use LEGO® minifigures in its refugee awareness work. The LEGO Group gave permission, and a campaign of ads and posters starring LEGO minifigures was created. "What's the Difference?" features twelve identical LEGO minifigures. Nine are labeled with nasty names such as "scum" and "vermin." The last three labels, "refugee," "you," and "me," force people to question the way they think about refugees.

Za Evropu míru bez jaderných zbraní (For a Europe of Peace Without Nuclear Weapons)

1981, Czech Republic

This poster was created in a period of history known as the Second Cold War. During this time, the relationship between the Soviet Union (a country made up of smaller countries, including Russia) and the West (led mainly by the United States and the UK) broke down to the point that many people thought we were on the brink of a nuclear war. In 1985 the new Soviet leader Mikhail Gorbachev promised to reduce these tensions. In 1990 he was awarded the Nobel Peace Prize for his efforts.

The Hungry Need Bread Not Bombs. Stop the Arms Trade.

Quaker Peace & Service
1981, UK

This poster was published by the Quakers, or Religious Society of Friends, a faith group committed to the promotion of equality and peace. The poster calls for an end to international trade in weapons, known as the arms trade.

The image conveys a powerful message about the effects of war and questions why a nation would choose to buy and sell weapons when its citizens need food. The bomb is drawn sliced to represent a loaf of bread, and the sheaf of wheat dominates the space to represent its importance.

War Is Not Healthy for Children and Other Living Things®

Designed by Lorraine Schneider for Another Mother for Peace
1969, USA

This poster was originally a Mother's Day card. A group of mothers protesting the Vietnam War sent the card to the US government. Inside the card they asked for "an end to killing" rather than the "candy or flowers" they usually received on Mother's Day. The group went on to form Another Mother for Peace, an organization that encourages women to make a stand against war.

PROTECT KIDS
DONT SHOOT
NOT GUNS
@MICAHBAZANT • @AMPLIFIERART • REGISTER TO VOTE! TEXT NVRAGAIN TO RTVOTE

YOUNG PEOPLE FOR CHANGE

> " If you don't make your voices heard in the real world, nothing will change. "
>
> *David Hogg, survivor of the Marjory Stoneman Douglas High School shooting*

Protect Kids Not Guns

Designed by Micah Bazant for Amplifier
2018, USA

This poster was designed in support of students organizing the March for Our Lives protests, which demanded stricter gun laws in the United States. The artist especially wanted to honor black youth, who have been fighting gun violence for generations.

There is a long history of young people standing up for their beliefs. Many student protests address problems with education, such as the cost or quality of teaching, but several have been about bigger issues, such as racism, war, and unfair governments. Often student protests happen because young people feel ignored by the older generation that makes the laws.

Some youth protests expose unfair treatment. In 1960 four teenagers in Greensboro, North Carolina, sat down and refused to leave a lunch counter reserved for white people only. Their protest sparked a series of sit-ins across the South. In 1965 students in Australia organized the Freedom Ride, a bus tour to bring attention to the racism suffered by Aboriginal people.

In 1968 there was an increase in student-led protests across the world. In France students fought for more freedom against a controlling government, inspiring eleven million factory workers to join their cause and demand better wages and working conditions.

Student protests have even helped overthrow powerful governments. During the Velvet Revolution of 1989—named for its peaceful nonviolence—students in what was then Czechoslovakia won the support of the country and succeeded in getting rid of a government that had ruled for more than forty years.

The Never Again campaign of 2018 was organized by American students fighting for safer gun laws. After seventeen people lost their lives in a school shooting in Florida, students helped organize school walkouts and demonstrations, including the March for Our Lives, held on March 24, 2018. The march called for the government to take school shootings seriously and make better laws to protect people from guns. Up to two million people participated, making it one of the biggest protests in American history, and one of the biggest youth protests since the Vietnam War. Although the students encountered significant political resistance, they did secure some changes to gun safety laws, and they continue to raise awareness of gun violence across the country.

Student protests fight for a fairer world. Even when young people can't yet vote for change, they can create change by inspiring those who can.

No Draft, No War, No Nukes

Designed by unknown artist
1970s, USA

This poster shows the Statue of Liberty, a symbol of freedom, holding a burning draft card. Draft cards are sent to tell people they have been called up to serve in the military. The first person to burn a draft card was twenty-two-year-old Eugene Keyes, who set fire to his card on Christmas Day 1963, in protest of the Vietnam War. University students in the United States were one of the first groups to protest against this war. Their activism inspired the broader public to join the anti-war movement.

The Occupied Wall Street Journal

Illustration by Matt Huynh
2011, USA

In 2009 students in California began to occupy campus buildings and roads to protest rising tuition costs and budget cuts. Their actions inspired others to protest against issues such as economic inequality, youth unemployment, and the unfair influence that large, rich companies have over government decisions.

Protesters across the United States joined what became known as the Occupy movement. They were united under the slogan "We are the 99 percent," referring to the increased concentration of wealth and power among the top 1 percent of income earners in the United States.

This poster was produced for Occupy Wall Street, which began on September 17, 2011, in Zuccotti Park, in New York City's Wall Street financial district. The protest continued for almost two months and sparked other Occupy protests in more than nine hundred cities across the world.

Malala Yousafzai

Syracuse Cultural Workers
2016, USA

This poster features a portrait of Malala Yousafzai, probably the best-known youth protester in recent times. Malala was born in Pakistan. When the local Taliban (a terrorist group) tried to ban girls from going to school, Malala stood up for girls' right to education. In retaliation, the Taliban shot her, but she survived. She was treated in the UK, where she also resumed her education.

On July 12, 2013, her sixteenth birthday, Malala spoke at the United Nations. She called for worldwide access to education, saying, "I am not against anyone. Neither am I here to speak in terms of personal revenge against the Taliban or any other terrorist group. I am here to speak up for the right of education for every child." It was her first speech since the shooting. July 12 was later declared Malala Day.

Global Climate Strike

Designed by Lisa Congdon for US Global Youth
Climate Strike
2019, USA

On March 15, 2019, students around the world walked out of classrooms to protest against climate change and their governments' delay in dealing with the problem. That global walkout has been followed by others in various countries. These climate strikes were inspired by sixteen-year-old Greta Thunberg from Sweden, who protests every Friday outside the Swedish parliament instead of going to school.

One child, one teacher, one book and one pen
can change the world
MALALA YOUSAFZAI

Malala Yousafzai, at age 17, became the youngest recipient of the Nobel Peace Prize in 2014.
An outspoken advocate of education for girls and all children, Malala left her native Pakistan following
an assassination attempt in 2012 by the Taliban. Since her recovery she has traveled the world
standing with oppressed peoples and encouraging them to claim their human rights.

P746CW   Artwork: Vecteezy.com, Design: SCW   Available as a framed poster, framed small print, notecard and postcard.
Web store/catalog · SyracuseCulturalWorkers.com · Box 6367, Syracuse NY 13217 USA · 800-949-5139   Printed by union labor on 30% postconsumer waste (PCW) recycled paper   12-18

nous sommes

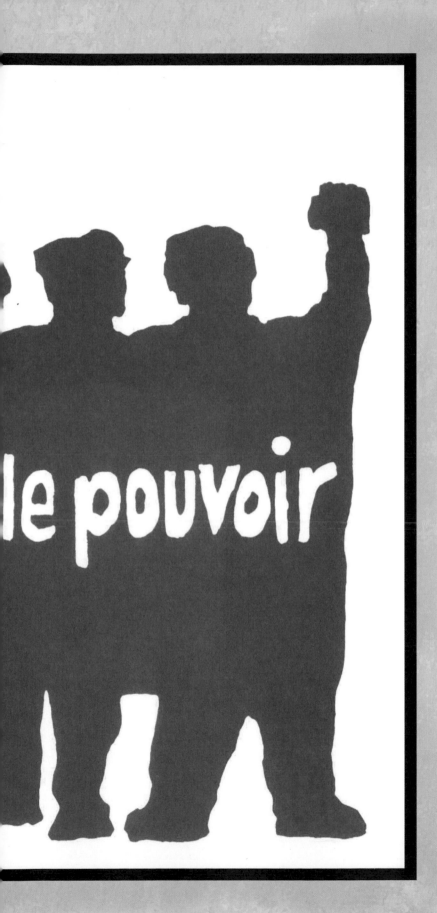

**Nous sommes le pouvoir
(We Are the Power)**

Designed by Atelier Populaire
1968, France

This poster was hand-printed by art
students in Paris to encourage factory
workers to join their protest against the
government. The raised fist is a common
symbol of solidarity and resistance.

SOME PEOPLE ARE GAY. GET OVER IT!

FREE TO LOVE

> "We should all speak out when someone is arrested and imprisoned because of who they love or how they look. This is one of the great, neglected human rights challenges of our time. "
>
> *Ban Ki-moon, former secretary-general of the United Nations*

We all have the right to be treated equally, but it is more difficult for some people than others because of the laws and rules in their countries. Many people around the world are still bullied, beaten, or even arrested because of how they look or whom they love.

Today there are thriving communities all over the world that support LGBTQ people. The acronym LGBTQ refers to lesbian women (who are attracted to other women), gay men (who are attracted to other men), bisexual people (who are attracted to more than one gender), transgender people (who identify as a different gender than the one they were assigned at birth), and those who are questioning their sexual orientation or gender identity. The *Q* also refers to those who identify as queer, a term intended to refer to anyone under the LGBTQ umbrella. Some members of the community consider the term *queer* to be a harmful slur because of how it was used in the past. Others have reclaimed the term as an inclusive way to refer to everyone in the community.

For a long time, LGBTQ people have been forced to hide who they really are due to prejudice and persecution. That is still true for many people, especially those in countries where there are laws that discriminate against them based on their sexual orientation or gender identity.

The fight for LGBTQ rights has been a long one. At the beginning of the twentieth century, many countries were hostile to the idea of people of the same gender having a loving relationship or

Some People Are Gay. Get Over It!

Designed for Stonewall
2007, UK

This poster was originally sent to every secondary school in England to help tackle the bullying of children who are gay, lesbian, or bisexual. It has since been seen on 600 billboards, 20 major train stations' advertising screens, and 3,500 bus panels.

getting married. Being gay, lesbian, bisexual, or transgender was even considered a mental illness! It wasn't until the 1960s that those protesting for equal rights started to see change.

Over the years the movement has focused on more protection for LGBTQ people within the law, so they are legally protected against hate crimes and have equal social rights, such as the right to marry whom they choose. In 2001 the Netherlands became the first country to allow people of the same sex to marry. The US Supreme Court declared same-sex marriage legal in 2015.

Today there are many countries that allow same-sex couples to marry, but there are still too many places in the world where LGBTQ people face severe consequences for wanting the freedom to love or marry whom they choose, or be who they are.

Equality Is a Human Right

Amnesty International
2016, UK

This poster takes a stand against behavior that is homophobic (against gay and lesbian people), transphobic (against people who are transgender), and biphobic (against people who love both men and women).

EQUALITY IS A HUMAN RIGHT

INTERNATIONAL DAY AGAINST
HOMOPHOBIA, TRANSPHOBIA & BIPHOBIA

AMNESTY INTERNATIONAL

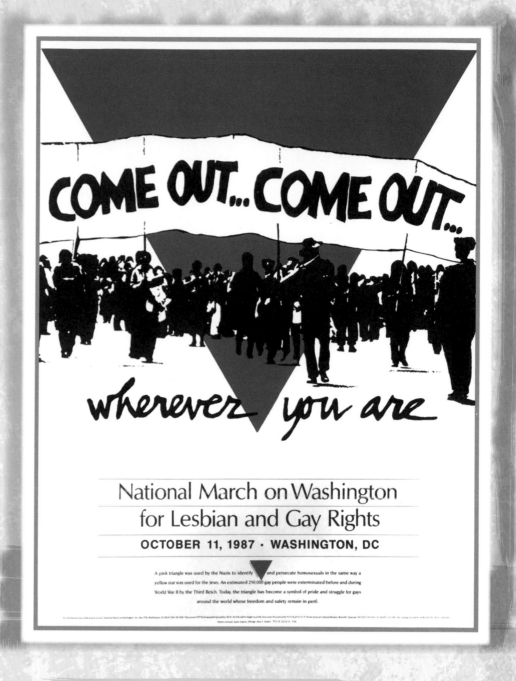

Come Out . . . Come Out . . . Wherever You Are

Designed by Jan Phillips, Amy Bartell, and Susie Gaynes
1987, USA

"Coming out" is a term used to describe the time when a person chooses to let others know they are gay, lesbian, bisexual, transgender, or non-binary. This poster features a pink triangle. During World War II the Nazis used it as a so-called "badge of shame" to identify gay men in concentration camps. The pink triangle has since been reclaimed by the LGBTQ community and is now a symbol of pride alongside the better-known rainbow flag.

art by rommy torrico

GENTE NO BINARIA EXISTE

NON BINARY PEOPLE EXIST

Gente no binaria existe/ Non Binary People Exist

Designed by Rommy Torrico for GLAAD
2018, USA

This poster was one of ten designed for a bilingual campaign called #InclusiveScreens for GLAAD, an organization that promotes the inclusion of LGBTQ people in the media.

Non-binary people do not identify as one gender or another. The poster calls for more fully developed non-binary characters and more on-screen roles for non-binary actors. It is particularly focused on those from ethnic minority groups, who are often overlooked and who rarely see themselves represented in the media.

Stonewall 25

Linda Malik and Dik Cool
with art by Harry Freeman-Jones
1994, USA

This poster commemorates the twenty-fifth anniversary of the 1969 Stonewall riots, a series of demonstrations held by the LGBTQ community in New York City to campaign for fair treatment. The Stonewall uprising was a spark for change and a defining moment in the history of LGBTQ rights. A year later a march organized by activist Brenda Howard was held to mark the first anniversary of Stonewall. This is now considered the first Gay Pride parade. Today Pride events take place all over the world to celebrate and support the fight for equal rights.

UNFORTUNATELY, HISTORY HAS SET THE RECORD A LITTLE TOO STRAIGHT.

James Baldwin/Writer
1924 - 1987

Willa Cather/Writer
1873 - 1947

Errol Flynn/Actor
1909 - 1959

Michelangelo/Artist
1475 - 1564

Edna St. Vincent Millay/Poet
1892 - 1950

Cole Porter/Composer
1891 - 1964

Eleanor Roosevelt/Social Activist
1884 - 1962

Bessie Smith/Singer
1894 - 1937

Walt Whitman/Poet
1819 - 1892

Virginia Woolf/Writer
1882 - 1941

A Little Too Straight

Laurie Casagrande for the Gay and
Lesbian Community Action Council
1988, USA

This poster features portraits of ten
famous people whose sexual orientation
was, at the time, left out of history books.
Its heading plays on the expression
"setting the record straight." When you
set the record straight, you correct
something that was previously wrong.
The word *straight* is also used to describe
people who are heterosexual (men who
are attracted to women, or women who
are attracted to men). The poster was
produced for the first National Coming
Out Day, in 1988. This is now an annual
event that takes place on October 11.

Back Home, It's a Crime to Show My Colours

Fondation Émergence
2018, Canada

Produced for the 2018 International Day
Against Homophobia and Transphobia
(May 17), this poster features the
rainbow flag, a symbol of pride for the
LGBTQ community since it was designed
by gay activist Gilbert Baker in the
1970s. The different colors of the flag
celebrate diversity. But for many people
throughout the world, "showing your
colors" (expressing your true beliefs or
personality) can mean a criminal charge
or worse. The man featured on this poster
is from Tunisia, where people can serve
up to three years in prison for being gay
or lesbian.

STAND TOGETHER FOR THE PLANET

"You cannot get through a single day without having an impact on the world around you. What you do makes a difference, and you have to decide what kind of difference you want to make."

Jane Goodall, primatologist

Concern for the environment isn't a recent issue. Some indigenous cultures have had environmental laws for millennia. It's hard to identify an exact moment when environmentalism started in Western society, but it was during the nineteenth century that laws to protect the earth were first made in Europe and the United States.

As the Industrial Revolution spread, a switch from handmade crafts to machine-manufactured goods meant factories sprang up across the world. They were powered by burning coal, which led to high levels of air pollution. Many people suffered health problems, and their protests eventually led to environmental laws.

By the mid-1970s, many people felt that the earth was on the edge of environmental disaster and wanted to do more to protect it. These individuals got together and set up organizations such as Greenpeace and Friends of the Earth—organizations that still exist today and have millions of supporters worldwide.

The biggest issue facing us now is climate change. When fossil fuels are burned, they produce carbon dioxide (CO_2) and other heat-trapping gases. If there is too much of this gas in the atmosphere, it causes the earth to get warmer. Global warming leads to climate change: changing weather patterns, rising sea levels, melting ice caps, and extreme events such as hurricanes, heat waves, forest fires, and flooding.

Non à l'autoroute Rive Gauche (No to the Left Bank Highway)
Designed by Raymond Savignac
c. 1972, France

This poster protesting against a highway in Paris shows Notre-Dame cathedral as a person drowning in a sea of cars. It sends an effective message about the dangers of pollution.

What's more, even though people in poorer countries produce less CO$_2$, they suffer much more from the effects of climate change. They may struggle to grow enough food because it's too hot or live in homes or shelters that can't withstand extreme weather like hurricanes and flooding. This isn't fair.

Our planet is also running out of fossil fuels. We must switch to "green" or "clean" technology—sources of renewable energy that produce less CO$_2$, such as solar power and wind farms.

There are solutions. New technology is being developed all the time, and it's getting cheaper, too. It's up to us to make sure that governments don't just make promises but also take action and make changes.

Shell. Own Up. Pay Up. Clean Up.

Amnesty International
2012, UK

Oil spills are common in Nigeria, an oil-producing country, and they have a huge impact on the people who live there. In 2008 two huge oil spills devastated Bodo Creek, in the Niger Delta, destroying the environment and with it the livelihoods of many locals who depend on fishing to support their families. The Shell oil company did eventually own up to the spills and agreed to pay more than $70 million in compensation. However, the pollution has never been cleaned up. The area remains devastated, with food shortages and polluted drinking water severely affecting the health of local people.

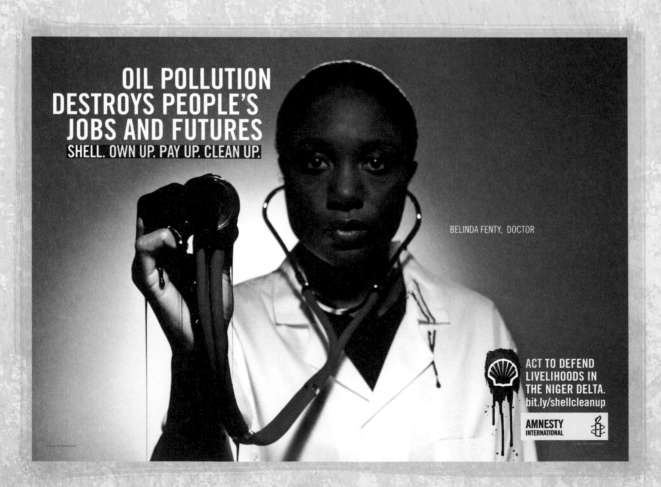

OIL POLLUTION DESTROYS PEOPLE'S JOBS AND FUTURES
SHELL. OWN UP. PAY UP. CLEAN UP.

BELINDA FENTY, DOCTOR

ACT TO DEFEND LIVELIHOODS IN THE NIGER DELTA.
bit.ly/shellcleanup

AMNESTY INTERNATIONAL

International Day of Action against Dams and for Rivers, Water and Life

Designed by Roberto Arroyo
2000s, USA

March 14 has been the International Day of Action for Rivers since 1997. The movement started in Brazil, where the building of dams caused many people to suffer. Dams damage the health of our rivers and the local environment and are responsible for the displacement of around two million people a year.

Killer Bags

Surfers Against Sewage
2014, UK

The plastic-bag fish seen here is a
reminder that we urgently need to deal
with the issue of plastic pollution.
Scientists have found that some
seabirds' stomachs are full of plastic
instead of food. We might be eating
plastic, too, when we eat fish that have
accidentally eaten microscopic bits
of plastic. It has been estimated that
unless we take action, by 2050 the
oceans will contain more plastic than
fish by weight.

PLASTIC FREE
C⊘ASTLINES
SURFERS AGAINST SEWAGE

Man needs rain forests too

The tropical rain forests are home to half of all the plant animal and insect species on earth, and are watersheds that prevent erosion drought and flooding. Help WWF save them from destruction.

WWF 🐼 WORLD WILDLIFE FUND Panda House 11–13 Ockford Road Godalming Surrey

Not Here But Now

Amnesty International
2006, Switzerland

This poster is from a series that places the issue of human rights quite literally in front of our eyes. More than two hundred posters were put up around Switzerland, each matching its surroundings to create the illusion that the scene in the poster was actually happening in front of the viewer.

This poster shows a boy scavenging for food and translates to "It's not happening here, but it is happening." It highlights the environmental problems that people in poorer countries suffer because of climate change. It is effective because it brings issues that are happening far away to our immediate attention and forces us to think about them.

Man Needs Rain Forests Too

Designed for the World Wildlife Fund by Tom Eckersley
1982, UK

This poster shows the importance of protecting rain forests. It was produced in 1982, when the Amazon rain forest was being destroyed at an alarming rate. Worldwide protests led to a dramatic decrease in destruction, but other rain forests still need our help. Animals such as orangutans, Borneo elephants, and Sumatran tigers are facing near-extinction. Their habitats are being cut down to make way for mining, illegal logging, and farms that produce palm oil, a substance found in many products, from cookies to soap and detergent.

ABOUT AMNESTY INTERNATIONAL

Human rights belong to every single one of us, wherever we live in the world, no matter who we are. They help us to live decent lives. They are defined and protected by law. Governments may not pick and choose which rights to respect or ignore.

Amnesty International is a global movement of millions of ordinary people standing up for humanity and human rights. We seek to protect people wherever human rights are denied. We support and engage in peaceful protest against oppression. We are proud to stand up for freedom.

We wholeheartedly support *Rise Up! The Art of Protest* because it shows how creativity and defiance can bring about positive change. The pictures in this book show a century of defiance—of brave people speaking truth to power. But it takes courage to protest and confidence to do so with flair.

Peaceful protest is part of making the world a better place. We hope this book inspires you to do the same whenever and wherever it is needed.

Find out more about the work of Amnesty International at **www.amnestyusa.org**.

Human Dignity, Human Rights

Amnesty International for the Demand Dignity campaign; photograph by Steve McCurry and design by Pentagram
2010, USA

This ten-year-old Afghan refugee lives in Peshawar, Pakistan, and has never seen her homeland.

HUMAN DIGNITY
HUMAN
RIGHTS

AMNESTY INTERNATIONAL

A TEN-YEAR OLD AFGHAN REFUGEE LIVING IN PESHAWAR, PAKISTAN. SHE HAS NEVER SEEN HER HOMELAND. PHOTO: STEVE MCCURRY/MAGNUM, 2002. PENTAGRAM DESIGN